Discover It Yourself

Flying and Floating

KINGFISHER
LONDON & NEW YORK

KINGFISHER

LONDON & NEW YORK

Published 2021 by Kingfisher
This edition published in 2023
Published in the United States by
Kingfisher, 120 Broadway,
New York, NY 10271
Kingfisher is an imprint of Macmillan
Children's Books, London
All rights reserved

Designed by Tall Tree
Illustrated by Diego Vaisberg/
Advocate Art

ISBN 978-0-7534-7672-7 (HB)
978-0-7534-7670-3 (PB)

Material previously published in
*Young Discoverers Flying and
Floating* (1993)

Library of Congress Cataloging-
in-Publication data has been
applied for.

EU representative: 1st Floor, The
Liffey Trust Centre, 117-126 Sheriff
Street Upper, Dublin 1 D01 YC43

Kingfisher books are available for
special promotions and
premiums. For details contact:
Special Markets Department,
Macmillan, 120 Broadway,
New York, NY 10271

Printed in China
9 8 7 6 5 4 3 2 1
1TR/1222/WKT/UG/128MA

Contents

Make sure you have a grown-up to help whenever you see this sign.

!

Air and Water

Air and water are essential for life on Earth. Without air to breathe and water to drink, we could not survive. But what exactly are air and water? Air and water have different properties—they look, feel, and behave in different ways. Air is a gas. You can't see it or taste it, but you can feel it when it blows over your face and hands. Water is usually a liquid, but it can also be a solid or a gas (see page 18).

Exosphere

Thermosphere

Mesosphere

Stratosphere

Troposphere

Without water and air, all animals and plants would die. Animals use oxygen gas from the air when they breathe in. Much of the oxygen in the air is replaced by green plants, which produce oxygen in their leaves when they make food.

The Atmosphere

The atmosphere is a layer of air around Earth. It is often divided into five bands—the troposphere (closest to Earth), stratosphere, mesosphere, thermosphere, and exosphere. Air is mostly made up of the two gases nitrogen (78%) and oxygen (21%). It also contains carbon dioxide gas (0.03%), water in the form of a gas (water vapor), and tiny bits of salt, dust, and dirt.

DISCOVER IT YOURSELF!

Try these four simple experiments to compare the properties of air and water.

Blow up one balloon and fill another with water, keeping it over the sink so you don't make a mess. To fill the water balloon, stretch the balloon's neck over the end of the faucet, then slowly turn on the water. Or you could use a funnel. Knot the end of each balloon.

1. First, hold one balloon in each hand to see which is heavier. You'll find that the balloon filled with water is much heavier than the one filled with air.

2. Now squeeze each balloon. The air balloon will be firm and taut and will feel a little springy. The one filled with water will change shape as the water sloshes around inside.

More than two-thirds of Earth's surface is covered with water. Pictures of the whole Earth usually show a side with land, but from another angle our planet looks blue.

3. Next, try sinking the balloons in water. You will be able to push the water-filled balloon under the water more easily than the air-filled balloon.

4. Finally, stick a pin in each balloon. The air balloon will pop as the air rushes out, but the water balloon will simply sag as the water trickles away.

The Weight of Air

Air has weight, even though it seems thin and light. For example, the air inside a bus weighs as much as one of the passengers! Air is one thousand times lighter than water. This means that the air in a bathtub weighs about the same as a cupful of water. Air also takes up space—see how air bubbles fill the bottle in the experiment below.

Blow It Up

When you pump up the tires on a bike, you're increasing the air pressure inside so that it can support both you and the bike (see next page).

DISCOVER IT YOURSELF!

Here's a fun way to measure how much air your lungs hold (and find out more about the properties of air). You'll need a bowl, a large plastic bottle, and a long tube.

1. Pour water into the bowl so it is three-fourths full. Then completely fill the bottle with water. Put your fingers over the top of the bottle so the water doesn't spill, turn it upside down, and lower it into the bowl.

2. Thread the tube into the neck of the bottle. Then take a deep breath and blow down the tube.

? How It Works

Air is lighter than water, and it takes up space. As you blow, air bubbles rise up the tube and push the water out of the neck of the bottle into the bowl.

The weight of all the air in Earth's atmosphere pushes on everything with a force called air pressure. It may be hard to believe, but the air pressing on every square inch of your body weighs almost 15 pounds (7 kg for every 6.5 cm²)! The reason you're not crushed by all that weight is because the air and liquids inside you push back with the same force.

Eye Spy

Have you ever sucked air from a plastic bottle or a thin metal can when you're drinking from it? Air pressure flattens the sides of the bottle or can slightly. The sides pop out again when you let air back in.

A drinking straw works by air pressure. When you suck air out of the straw, air pressure on the surface of the drink pushes the liquid up into your mouth.

The amount of air in the atmosphere varies—the higher you go, the less there is. We describe this as the air getting thinner. Climbers of very high mountains, such as Mount Everest, must carry tanks of oxygen with them so they can still breathe.

Hot Air

Have you ever wondered why smoke from a fire goes up into the air rather than spreading out sideways? The reason is that hot air is lighter than cold air, so hot air rises. Rising hot air is used to lift huge air balloons. A hot-air balloon is simply a large bag made out of a light material. The air inside a hot-air balloon is heated by a gas burner. This makes the balloon float up into the cooler atmosphere.

Lighter Than Air

Some gases, such as helium, are lighter than air. This means that they don't need to be heated to help things fly. Helium-filled blimps are sometimes used for advertising and aerial observation.

DISCOVER IT YOURSELF!

Make a hot-air pinwheel and balloon to see how hot air rises.

Hot-Air Pinwheel

1. Cut out a circle of cardboard and make eight cuts, as shown. Twist up the edges slightly (so that air can rise through the gaps).

2. Push a pin through the middle of the cardboard to make a hole. Thread string through the hole and knot the end. (Make a large knot so the string doesn't slip through.)

3. Dangle the pinwheel over a rising current of hot air (from a radiator, for example, or a large cup of coffee), and watch it spin.

Hot-Air Balloon

1. Cut out eight 2-foot-long (60 cm) pieces of tissue paper in the shape shown.

2. Glue the edges together to make a balloon shape. Don't use too much glue or your balloon will be too heavy.

3. Fill the balloon with hot air from a hair dryer. Does it fly? You could make a small tissue paper box and tie it to the bottom of the balloon to see whether the balloon can carry a load.

The Force of the Wind

When hot air rises, cool air usually flows in to take its place. This is what makes the wind blow. During the day, the Sun heats up parts of the land and the ocean, which then warm the air above them. This warm air rises into the atmosphere and a stream of cooler air—the wind—blows in. Winds carry seeds, make flags flap, and fill sails on boats. Strong winds can knock down trees and buildings.

Eye Spy

Look out for things that are moved by the push of the wind. Wind socks show which way the wind is blowing. Seeds are spread by the wind.

Beaufort Scale

In 1805, a British admiral named Sir Francis Beaufort introduced a scale to show the effect of different wind strengths on sailing ships at sea.

Today, the Beaufort scale describes the strength of the wind on land as well as at sea. The scale has 12 numbers, ranging from calm to a violent hurricane.

Force 0 Calm	Forces 1–3 Light breeze	Forces 4–5 Moderate wind	Forces 6–7 Strong wind	Forces 8–9 Gale	Forces 10–11 Storm	Force 12 Hurricane
Smoke goes straight up	Leaves rustle; small branches move	Small trees sway	Large trees sway	Tiles fall off roofs	Widespread damage	Disaster

Most things are heavier than air, so they do not float upward on a still day. But on a windy day, the wind can carry some lightweight things into the sky. This is how a kite works—it's lifted by the force of the wind.

DISCOVER IT YOURSELF!

Make a kite! You'll need a large piece of strong plastic (cut from a bag), two light sticks or lengths of dowel, tape, and strong string.

1. Open out the plastic and ask an adult to cut it in the shape and size shown. Cut out a triangular hole (a vent) and strengthen the corners with tape.

2. Tape the sticks and a piece of string to the plastic, and then tie on a long string to hold.

WARNING!

NEVER FLY YOUR KITE NEAR OVERHEAD POWER LINES.

Flying Hints

First choose a windy day! Unwind your string about 3 feet (1 m). You may need to run into the breeze to start with. Let the string out as the kite starts to lift.

Gliding Through the Air

Hot-air balloons and kites fly because they are lighter than air. But most aircraft are heavier than air. They need wings to help them fly. Wings are a special shape—they're curved more above than below. They work when they move through the air at just the right angle. The flow of air above and below the wing makes a force called lift, which keeps the aircraft in the air.

1

Many birds push themselves into the air by flapping their broad, flat wings. Some birds, such as gulls, soar and glide on moving air currents.

Using Thermals

Thermals are created when dark surfaces, such as roads and fields, soak up heat from the Sun and then pass on the heat to the air above. Gliders and soaring birds use these rising warm air currents to fly higher and stay airborne longer.

2

Hang gliders are usually launched by running down slopes or jumping off cliffs.

When you ride your bicycle fast, you can feel the air rushing past your body. But the faster you go, the more the air drags you back. Modern cars and aircraft are smooth and rounded so that they pass through the air with as little drag, or air resistance, as possible.

4

Parachutes fall rather than fly. The open parachute fills with air and works like a brake, using the air's drag to slow itself down.

Gliders drift slowly downward at a gentle angle unless the pilot can find a rising air current to carry the lightweight glider up again.

3

DISCOVER IT YOURSELF!
Check how the flow of air acts on a wing, making lift.

Find a thin sheet of paper and hold it just under your lips. Blow hard over the paper and watch what happens. You'll find that the paper will lift. The air you have blown over the paper moved faster and had less pressure than the air under the paper. This difference in air pressure made the paper lift.

Staying Up

All aircraft with wings will only fly if they can move fast enough to keep air flowing around their wings (making lift). They also need enough lift to overcome their weight.

DISCOVER IT YOURSELF!

Make a toy parachute and glider!

Toy parachute

1. Cut a square of plastic from a plastic bag or some fine, lightweight material. Make a small hole in the center. (This makes the parachute more stable.)

2. Tape a thread to each corner of the parachute.

3. Tie the free ends of the threads together and tape the knot to a toy figurine. Roll the parachute into a ball and toss it into the air.

Superglider

1. Fold a sheet of rectangular paper in half, making a neat, stiff crease down the middle. Fold up the front edge two or three times.

2. Fold the back edge once and make a series of cuts (for flaps), as shown. Launch the glider into the air. If it falls too fast, unfold some of the paper from the front. If it stalls (tips up at the front and then dips down), add more folds at the front. Bend the flaps to see how they change the glider's flight.

3. Try some of these glider shapes, or design your own.

Planes and Helicopters

Because they can hover, helicopters are useful for watching traffic, lifting loads, and rescuing people from oceans and mountainsides.

Gliders and hang gliders must go where air currents take them, but aircraft with engines can travel where the pilot wishes, and they can keep going until they run out of fuel. Engines keep an airplane pushing through the air so that its wings are working, creating lift. Helicopters are different because they can fly backward, forward, and up and down. They create lift by pushing down on the air. Tilting the blades moves the helicopter in different directions.

DISCOVER IT YOURSELF!

Make a helicopter rotor.

1. Ask an adult to cut a rectangular strip from a plastic bottle.

2. Cut two slits, one on each side of the strip, as shown.

3. Make a small hole in the middle of the strip and push a pencil through it so that it's a tight fit.

4. Hold the pencil between the palms of your hands, spin it quickly, and let go.

Wind Power

Did you know that there is more energy in a gale than a city uses in a year? For hundreds of years, people have used the power of the wind to sail ships or to turn windmill sails to grind corn. Wind power can be used to make electricity, too. Unlike coal and oil, wind power does not involve burning fuel and releasing gases that harm the planet.

Sailing Ships

The huge square sails on this old sailing ship were designed to catch the wind coming from behind. This is called sailing before the wind.

DISCOVER IT YOURSELF!

Experiment with sails.

Make three or four model boats from plastic containers or empty juice boxes. Using colored paper, cut different sail shapes and sizes and attach them to straws using sticky tape. Stick the sail to the inside of your boat using modeling clay. Float the boats on water and blow them along with a straw to see which one has the best sail.

DISCOVER IT YOURSELF!

Make a pinwheel windmill with a square of thick paper, a straw, a pin, and glue.

1. Make four cuts in the thick paper, as shown.

2. Fold over the edges and glue them in place.

3. Cut a short piece off the end of the straw. Push a pin through the center of the paper, the short straw, and the longer straw. Ask an adult to bend the back of the pin over.

A Watery World

We drink it, we wash with it, we swim in it—water is very special. Without water, Earth would be a dry, lifeless desert. Water can exist in three different forms—as a liquid, as a gas (called water vapor), and as a solid (ice), and we use all three forms of water in our everyday lives. For example, steam irons use the gas from boiling water to press clothes, and we have iced drinks to keep cool.

Water freezes at 32°F (0°C) and boils at 212°F (100°C). Steam is a cloud of water droplets. Steam spurts from a boiling kettle because it takes up more space than the liquid.

Frozen Solid

Solid water forms in two different ways. Ice is made when liquid water cools to 32°F (0°C). This temperature is called water's "freezing point." The second way is when vapor freezes to make frost. For example, dew may freeze into frost on cold mornings.

Gravity, the invisible force that pulls everything toward the center of Earth, pulls on water, too. In places where it cannot flow through surface rocks, water forms rivers, lakes, and oceans. In other places, different kinds of rock let the water seep through. All water on Earth eventually settles at the lowest level that it can possibly reach.

DISCOVER IT YOURSELF!

See how the surface of water in any container is always level, no matter which way you tilt it. You'll need two clear plastic bottles with tops and a plastic tube.

1. Fill one of the bottles with water and screw on the top.

2. Connect the bottles with the plastic tube. Use shampoo or ketchup bottles with conical nozzles, over which you can push the tube, or ask an adult to make holes through the bottle tops for you.

3. Turn the bottles upside down. Make a small hole in the bottom of each bottle to let the air in and out. Now change the height of the bottles and compare the water levels.

? How It Works

You'll find that no matter where you hold the bottles, the water will flow from one to the other until the level of water is the same in both of them.

Water Pressure

Can you swim under water? If so, perhaps you have felt pressure in your ears as you swim near the bottom of the pool. This pressure is caused by the weight of the water above you, pushing against you and into your ears. At the bottom of deep oceans, the water pressure is so enormous that it would crush your body. Yet there are some strange creatures that can survive there.

Life in the Deep

The Sun's light and heat cannot reach deep down in the oceans, so it's dark and cold there. The deep-sea anglerfish carries its own small light in front of its mouth to attract its prey. Some deep-sea fish are actually held together by water pressure, and most die when they are brought up from the deep.

Some strong steel submersibles, like *Alvin*, are specially designed so that they can dive to depths of 13,000 feet (4,000 m) and explore the ocean floor.

DISCOVER IT YOURSELF!

Make a bubble diver. You'll need a clear plastic bottle with a screw top, a plastic pen top, and some modeling clay.

1. Stick a small piece of modeling clay to the long stick part of the pen top. This is your diver. Test the diver in a glass of water to make sure it floats properly. The diver should just float at the water's surface, as shown on the right. If it floats too high, add some more clay. If it sinks, remove some clay.

2. Fill the bottle with water all the way up to the brim. Drop the diver in the bottle and screw on the top.

3. To make it dive, squeeze the bottle. To make it surface, release the pressure.

If your "diver" has a hole in the top, fill it with clay to make it watertight.

Eye Spy

Cut about five holes in the side of a plastic bottle and then fill the bottle with water. See how water pressure makes the water from the bottom hole squirt out the farthest.

Put a strip of tape over the holes and then peel it off when the bottle is full.

? How It Works

When you lower the diver into the water, a bubble of air gets trapped inside the pen top. Squeezing the bottle increases the water pressure, making the air bubble smaller, and the diver sinks. When you let go, the bubble gets bigger again and the diver rises.

Floating and Sinking

Have you ever wondered why some things float on water while other things sink? A plastic ball will float, for example, but a stone will sink at once. Whether something floats or sinks depends on its density (how heavy it is for its size) and its shape. The shape of an object controls how much water it pushes out of the way, or displaces. A plastic ball floats because it is lighter than water. It cannot displace much water with its weight. A stone is heavier than water, so its weight pulls it under.

Density

A cube of iron is seven times heavier than a cube of water the same size. But a cube of balsa wood is five times lighter than the water. If something is heavy for its size, we say it has a high density. If it is light for its size, it has a low density.

Eye Spy

Next time you take a bath, see how far the water level rises as you lower your body into the water. This will show you how much water you displace!

DISCOVER IT YOURSELF!

Experiment with different materials to see whether they float or sink. Then try changing sinkers to floaters.

First test a collection of solid objects, such as things made of metal, wood, glass, and plastic.

You'll find that small, heavy objects, such as coins and marbles, will sink. Larger, light things, such as a stick or a cork, will float.

Next, scrunch up a sheet of aluminum foil into a tight ball and drop it into the water. The ball will sink because it's heavier than the water it displaces. Now fold another sheet of foil into a boat shape. Does it float or sink now?

Try the same experiment with a ball of modeling clay.

? How It Works

The wide, flat boat shape displaces more water than the solid ball made from the same material. Most of the boat is actually filled with air. Together, the boat and the air inside it are lighter than the water they displace, so the boat floats.

Sometimes boats capsize—they turn on their sides and fill with water. To reduce this risk, a boat must be made in the right shape and its cargo must be loaded correctly so that the boat is balanced. Container ships like the one on the right are designed to carry heavy loads.

DISCOVER IT YOURSELF!

See which boat designs are best at carrying cargo safely.

1. Float a foil dish on some water. Add some marbles one at a time for the cargo. You'll find that the marbles roll around in the boat until they tip it over altogether.

2. Divide up the inside with strips of cardboard to make the cargo more stable. Large container ships, like the one in the picture above, are divided in a similar way.

3. Tape two foil trays side by side and balance the cargo again. This boat design is called a catamaran. It is a very stable design and will not capsize easily.

A Stretchy Skin

Some lightweight animals, such as this spider, use surface tension to walk on water.

Have you ever noticed how water collects into tiny drops on a polished car or on shiny shoes? The weight of the water tries to make it flow and spread, but water has a kind of stretchy elastic skin that holds it together. Fill a glass all the way up to the top with water. Can you see how the water's surface bulges slightly over the brim of the glass? The force holding the water together is surface tension.

DISCOVER IT YOURSELF!

A metal needle has a higher density than water and should sink, but you can make it float on water's stretchy skin.

Slowly slide a needle across the rim of a filled glass, onto the water's surface. Be careful not to break the surface tension. If you find this hard, try floating the needle on a raft of tissue paper. The paper will become waterlogged and sink, leaving the needle floating on the water.

Look closely—you'll be able to see how the water's skin flexes under the weight of the needle.

More Things to Try

Add one or two drops of liquid soap to the water. You'll find that the needle will soon drop to the bottom of the glass as the soap weakens the water's surface tension. This property of soap is used in the experiment on the next page.

25

DISCOVER IT YOURSELF!

Make a soap-powered boat. You will need some balsa wood and a tiny piece of hard soap.

1. Ask an adult to help you cut out the balsa wood in the shape shown in the circled drawing.

2. Fill a bowl with water, making sure that the water and the bowl are clean.

3. Push a small piece of soap into the triangular notch at the back of the boat and see how the boat is pulled forward.

? How It Works

As the soap weakens the surface tension at the back of the boat, the boat floats forward, pulled by the stronger surface tension in front.

Blowing Bubbles

By lowering water's surface tension, soap can make it even more stretchy. That's why you can blow bubbles with soapy water. Here's a good recipe for soap bubbles.

Gently stir four tablespoons of dish soap into two pints of water.

Stir in one teaspoon of white sugar.

Dip your bubble wand into the mixture and start blowing bubbles!

Puddles and Clouds

You can sometimes see water vapor rising from a damp dog as it lies steaming in the sunshine on a hot day.

Next time it rains, wait for the rain to stop, and then go out and see how long it takes for the rain puddles to disappear. Some of the water in puddles soaks down into the ground, but the rest dries up into the air. The Sun's heat makes the water turn into the gas we call water vapor. This process is called evaporation. Water evaporates more quickly when there is a breeze blowing than when the air is still. That's why laundry hung outside dries faster on a windy day than on a still one.

DISCOVER IT YOURSELF!

Investigate how quickly water evaporates.

Find three pieces of cloth of equal size. Soak them in water and then leave them in different places to dry:

1. Hang the first on a line.

2. Leave the second wadded up in a bowl.

3. Lay the third flat on the ground.

Which one dries the fastest?

? ## How It Works

The cloth on the line will dry the fastest because the water vapor can escape from it more easily. If there's a breeze to carry the vapor away, the cloth will dry even more quickly.

Condensation

Water vapor in the air can turn back into liquid water, too. This happens when warm air cools down. As cold air cannot hold as much water vapor as warm air, some of the water vapor forms tiny drops of liquid. This process of gas turning back into liquid is called condensation. There is water vapor in the air you breathe out. If you breathe onto a cold glass mirror, some of the vapor in your breath condenses into a mist of tiny water droplets.

Clouds are made of water vapor. When warm air rises, it eventually cools and the water vapor condenses into a mist of droplets. If the droplets get large enough, they fall from the sky and it rains.

DISCOVER IT YOURSELF!

Leave some glasses in a freezer for about two minutes. When you bring them out, see how water vapor from the air condenses on their sides.

Eye Spy

Look out for water vapor condensing. You can often see it on the cool windows of a warm room, on the mirror of a steamy bathroom, or on the inside of a greenhouse. Plants give off water vapor at night (with carbon dioxide), which condenses on the greenhouse's cool glass.

Water Wheels

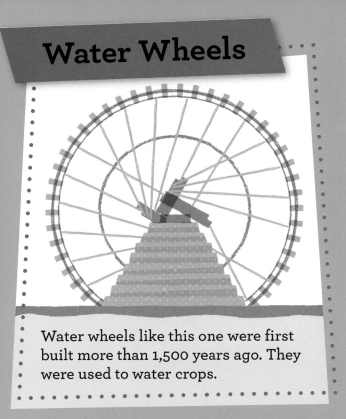

Water wheels like this one were first built more than 1,500 years ago. They were used to water crops.

We can use the power of moving water just as we can use wind power. Turning water wheels were once used to grind corn or to drive tools such as drills. Today, water power is used mostly to make electricity. Water is stored in huge reservoirs behind dams. When it is released, the force of the falling water drives turbines, which produce electrical power.

DISCOVER IT YOURSELF!

Build a water wheel.

1. Ask an adult to help you make a hole through the middle of a cork and cut eight slots in its sides.

2. Glue a small disposable wooden spoon in each slot. When the glue is dry, slide a knitting needle through the hole in the cork.

3. To work the wheel, hold it under a stream of gently running water.

Clean Air, Clean Water

We must have clean air to breathe and clean water to drink to stay healthy. Pollution is the dirtying of our land, air, and water. Air pollution comes from dangerous gases given off by factory chimneys and by car and aircraft exhausts. These gases mix with the water vapor in the air to make acid rain. Acid rain harms our land and water and poisons plants and animals.

Greenhouse Effect

This is a warming of Earth's climate by some gases that act like the glass windows of a greenhouse, trapping heat inside the atmosphere. Carbon dioxide is a greenhouse gas.

DISCOVER IT YOURSELF!

Test for air pollution around your home.

1. Find three shiny metal tin lids or small mirrors. These will be your dirt traps. Polish them with a clean, dry cloth, then smear a little petroleum jelly in the center of each.

2. Leave each dirt trap in a different place. For example, leave one inside, in a living room or a bedroom; one in a window box or a yard; and one near a busy road.

3. After a few days, collect your dirt traps and compare the amount of dirt they have collected. Which is the most polluted place?

? What you can do

Here are some ways to make the air cleaner for yourself and for others:

- Don't burn gardening waste—make it into compost.
- Buy products that are environment-friendly.
- Travel by bike or bus for short trips, rather than by car.

The water we drink is filtered and cleaned at water treatment plants before we use it. But much of Earth's water gets polluted by factory waste, by sewage, and by all the trash that careless people dump in our oceans, rivers, and lakes.

DISCOVER IT YOURSELF!

1. Soak soil and leaves in some water to make it muddy, then pour it through a mesh strainer.

2. Put a paper coffee filter in a funnel. Place a small cotton ball in the neck, then add some fine, clean sand.

3. Pour in some of your muddy water and see how the filter helps trap some of the dirt.

Eye Spy

Take a look at any ponds and rivers near your home—are they polluted with trash, or do they look clean and healthy? Help the environment by never throwing trash into lakes and streams.

? How It Works

The larger pieces of dirt get trapped in the cotton ball, sand, and coffee filter, letting cleaner water pass through. Don't drink it, though—it's still very dirty!

Index